CATS SET VI

JAPANESE BOBTAIL CATS

Jill C. Wheeler
ABDO Publishing Company

visit us at
www.abdopublishing.com

Published by ABDO Publishing Company, PO Box 398166, Minneapolis, MN 55439. Copyright © 2012 by Abdo Consulting Group, Inc. International copyrights reserved in all countries. No part of this book may be reproduced in any form without written permission from the publisher. The Checkerboard Library™ is a trademark and logo of ABDO Publishing Company.

Printed in the United States of America, North Mankato, Minnesota.
102011
012012

 PRINTED ON RECYCLED PAPER

Cover Photo: Photo by Helmi Flick
Interior Photos: Alamy p. 19; Animal Photography p. 21; AP Images p. 5; Corbis p. 9;
    Getty Images p. 10; Photos by Helmi Flick pp. 7, 11, 13, 15; Peter Arnold p. 17

Editors: Megan M. Gunderson, BreAnn Rumsch
Art Direction: Neil Klinepier

Library of Congress Cataloging-in-Publication Data

Wheeler, Jill C., 1964-
  Japanese bobtail cats / Jill C. Wheeler.
     p. cm. -- (Cats)
  Includes index.
  ISBN 978-1-61783-242-0
  1. Japanese bobtail cat--Juvenile literature. I. Title.
  SF449.J37W44 2012
  636.822--dc23
                         2011026473

CONTENTS

Lions, Tigers, and Cats 4

Japanese Bobtail Cats 6

Qualities 8

Coat and Color. 10

Size 12

Care 14

Feeding 16

Kittens. 18

Buying a Kitten 20

Glossary 22

Web Sites. 23

Index 24

LIONS, TIGERS, AND CATS

Long ago, wildcats and people discovered an important partnership. The cats quickly learned that human settlements offered lots of rats and mice to eat. And, humans learned these wildcats could protect their grain from such **rodents**.

Scientists believe people began **domesticating** cats in Egypt about 3,500 years ago. The practice then spread around the world. Eventually, humans began **breeding** cats with desirable qualities.

Today, there are more than 40 different breeds of domestic cats worldwide. These small cats share many features with the big cats in the zoo. That is because all cats are members of the family **Felidae**.

In the United States, **domestic** cats are the second most popular pet, after dogs. A favorite **breed** of cat lovers everywhere is the distinctive Japanese bobtail cat.

Japanese bobtails are one of the oldest cat breeds. Japanese artwork shows that the short tail has been common since at least the 1400s.

JAPANESE BOBTAIL CATS

Japanese bobtail cats are best known for their short pom-pom tails. No one knows how they came to have these **unique** tails. But, Japan is an island nation. The island kept the cats isolated, which allowed the mutation to develop in their population.

About AD 1600, these short-tailed felines helped save the nation's silk industry. Leaders ordered that all pet cats be released into the streets. Free to roam, the cats killed the **rodents** that had been eating the precious silkworms.

Yet, this freedom also meant that pet cats suddenly had to survive without human help. Only the strongest, smartest, and bravest adapted. They passed these qualities on to their descendants.

Then during the 1960s, Americans serving in the military in Japan discovered the Japanese bobtail. In 1968, Elizabeth Freret imported three for her US **breeding** program. By 1976, the breed had gained full recognition by the **Cat Fanciers' Association**.

Japanese legend tells how the bobtail came to be. One night, a sleeping cat's tail caught fire. It ran through the city streets, lighting houses on fire. Later, the emperor ordered that all cat tails be cut short to prevent another disaster!

QUALITIES

The Japanese bobtail cat is ideal for people seeking an active, affectionate family member. It has a loving, outgoing personality. This high-energy **breed** loves to play and is especially good with children.

Bobtails are at their best with constant companionship. They enjoy when their humans talk to them. They may talk back with chirping sounds in a range of tones.

Yet, Japanese bobtails are not lap cats! Instead, these bright felines like to keep busy hiding and exploring. Inquisitive and alert, these cats also remain masters of the pounce. So, they are skilled hunters.

Can someone be home all day with your bobtail? If not, provide this high-spirited animal with the company of another cat, dog, or other pet.

Japanese bobtails get along well with other cats. However, multiple bobtails in one house may form a separate group from other cat **breeds**.

Bobtails are intelligent and fearless. They like to carry things in their mouths and ride on their owners' shoulders.

COAT AND COLOR

Most Japanese bobtail cats have a soft, medium-length coat. The coat feels silky and lies

smooth against the body. However, some Japanese bobtails are long-haired. Their soft coats feature belly shag and fluff on their legs and neck. The leg hair is called britches and the neck hair is called ruff.

Short or long, Japanese bobtail coats come in many different colors and patterns.

The Japanese bobtail cat is the basis for the popular "good luck cat" or "beckoning cat" statues called **maneki-neko.** *These statues are often seen in Asian restaurants and stores.*

In Japanese **culture**, the mi-ke (mee-KAY) coat is considered luckiest. *Mi-ke* means "three-fur" in Japanese.

Tabby bobtails are white with brown, red, blue, cream, or silver striping. Japanese bobtails can also have **tortoiseshell** fur. Or, the fur can be solid black, blue, red, cream, or white.

Japanese bobtails may have gold eyes or green eyes. Yet, most of these cats are blue-eyed or odd-eyed. Odd-eyed bobtails have one blue eye and one gold eye.

The most common mi-ke combination is white fur with red and black splotches.

SIZE

Japanese bobtail cats are medium sized with a graceful appearance. They weigh from six to nine pounds (2.5 to 4 kg) when fully mature. Females are slightly smaller than males.

Most people identify the Japanese bobtail by its **unique** tail. The tail actually grows to about four to five inches (10 to 12.7 cm) long. However, it is kinked or curved to about three inches (7.6 cm) from the cat's body. Though the tail is curled, the cat can wiggle it expressively.

The bobtail's head is triangle-shaped with large, upright ears. The ears tip forward as though the cat is listening. The colorful eyes are large, oval, and slanted. The high cheekbones and defined whisker pads give the cat's face its shape.

Each bobtail's tail is as unique as a human fingerprint.

The Japanese bobtail cat's hind legs are longer than its front legs. However, the hind legs are angled so that the cat's back remains straight. All four legs end in oval paws.

CARE

Japanese bobtail cats are easy pets to care for. The **breed** is not known for any particular health problems. Like all cats, they require a visit to the veterinarian for a checkup and **vaccines** each year.

However, their tails are sensitive and should be handled gently. Parents of small children will need to make this clear. Everyone needs to be careful around kitty's tail.

Compared to other breeds, the bobtail's sleek coat is less likely to **mat** or tangle. Still, it does require grooming to remove dead hair and encourage new growth.

Once in a while, give your Japanese bobtail a bath. Remember to also keep its claws clipped and its eyes and ears clean.

Shorthair bobtails need only an occasional combing, while longhair bobtails need weekly grooming.

Indoors, cats need a few items to keep them comfortable. Provide a **litter box** and be sure to keep it clean. Lots of toys will help keep these skilled mousers busy. And, a scratching post will allow your cat to sharpen its claws.

FEEDING

Like all cats, Japanese bobtails are meat eaters. Today's high-quality cat foods provide a more balanced diet than one that contains just meat. These complete pet foods can be purchased in dry, moist, and semimoist forms.

Water is another important part of your cat's diet. Be sure to put out fresh water each day for your bobtail.

By now you know that Japanese bobtails are very active. So, weight gain is not usually a concern for this **breed**. However, bobtails do love treats. Too many can be unhealthy for any animal. So use good judgement when deciding how often to offer special snacks.

**A proper diet will keep your cat's coat
looking healthy and smooth!**

KITTENS

Japanese bobtails mature more quickly than many other **breeds**. As a result, these cats may become parents earlier than others. Japanese bobtail females are **pregnant** for about 65 days. A **litter** usually includes three or four kittens.

Newborns are larger than those of many other breeds. Still, they are born blind and deaf. Their senses begin to function after seven to ten days. After nine or ten weeks, the kittens should be ready to leave their mother.

New owners have much to plan for! This adventurous breed loves to explore. So homes should be prepared for a new kitten's acrobatics. This means putting away any items that could harm the cat.

Japanese bobtails should get used to grooming at an early age. This **breed** enjoys water. So prepare for bath time to turn into playtime! It is also a good idea to **spay** or **neuter** bobtail kittens early if they will not be bred.

Japanese bobtails are never born tailless or with full length tails.

BUYING A KITTEN

Japanese bobtail cats are still relatively rare in the United States. Once you locate a **breeder**, you may be placed on a waiting list. It is always best to work with a reputable breeder. They strive to keep their cats happy and healthy.

Consider your reasons for getting a bobtail before deciding how much to spend. Remember that show-quality cats are more expensive than pet-quality cats.

Now it's time to choose your kitten! A healthy kitten should look strong and alert. Its eyes and ears should be clean, and its nose should feel cool.

Is your kitten old enough to go home with you? By this time, it should know how to use a **litter box**. It should also have had its first **vaccines**.

And, the **breeder** should have started **socializing** it. Once home, you will need to continue introducing your kitten to new things.

Japanese bobtails make loyal and comforting friends. If well cared for, these cats should live about 9 to 13 years.

Is a Japanese bobtail the right cat breed for you?

GLOSSARY

breed - a group of animals sharing the same ancestors and appearance. A breeder is a person who raises animals. Raising animals is often called breeding them.

Cat Fanciers' Association - a group that sets the standards for judging all breeds of cats.

culture - the customs, arts, and tools of a nation or a people at a certain time.

domesticate - to adapt something to life with humans. Something domestic is tame, especially relating to animals.

Felidae (FEHL-uh-dee) - the scientific Latin name for the cat family. Members of this family are called felids. They include lions, tigers, leopards, jaguars, cougars, wildcats, lynx, cheetahs, and domestic cats.

litter - all of the kittens born at one time to a mother cat.

litter box - a box filled with cat litter, which is similar to sand. Cats use litter boxes to bury their waste.

mat - to form into a tangled mass.

neuter (NOO-tuhr) - to remove a male animal's reproductive glands.

pregnant - having one or more babies growing within the body.

rodent - any of several related animals that have large front teeth for gnawing. Common rodents include mice, squirrels, and beavers.

socialize - to adapt an animal to behaving properly around people or other animals in various settings.

spay - to remove a female animal's reproductive organs.

tabby - a coat pattern featuring stripes or splotches of a dark color on a lighter background. Individual hairs are banded with light and dark colors.

tortoiseshell - a coat pattern featuring patches of black, orange, and cream.

unique - being the only one of its kind.

vaccine (vak-SEEN) - a shot given to prevent illness or disease.

WEB SITES

To learn more about Japanese bobtail cats, visit ABDO Publishing Company online. Web sites about Japanese bobtail cats are featured on our Book Links page. These links are routinely monitored and updated to provide the most current information available.

www.abdopublishing.com

INDEX

A
adoption 18, 20

B
body 10, 12, 13
breeder 4, 7, 20, 21

C
care 8, 14, 15, 16,
    18, 19, 21
Cat Fanciers'
    Association 7
character 6, 7, 8, 9,
    12, 15, 16, 18, 20,
    21
claws 14, 15
coat 10, 11, 14
color 10, 11, 12

E
ears 12, 14, 20
eyes 11, 12, 14, 20

F
Felidae (family) 4
food 16
Freret, Elizabeth 7

G
grooming 14, 19

H
head 12
health 14, 16, 20
history 4, 6, 7
hunting 6, 8, 15

J
Japan 6, 7, 11

K
kittens 18, 19, 20,
    21

L
legs 10, 13
life span 21
litter box 15, 20

N
neuter 19
nose 20

P
paws 13

R
reproduction 18, 19

S
safety 18
scratching post 15
senses 18
size 6, 10, 12, 13, 18
socialization 21
spay 19

T
tail 6, 12, 14
toys 15
training 20

U
United States 5, 7, 20

V
vaccines 14, 20
veterinarian 14
voice 8

W
water 16
whisker pads 12